Fifty Feminist Mantras

a yearlong mantra practice for cultivating feminist consciousness

Text by Amelia Hruby
ameliahruby.com

Cover design by Emily Jones

ISBN: 1977845276
ISBN-13: 978-1977845276

To your feminine self, your feminist potential, and every woman* who's inspired or supported you along the way.

*Any time I say "woman" or "women" in this book, I mean anyone who identifies as a woman or with communities of women. I also mean the socially-constructed, structurally-oppressed position that produces concrete experiences of discrimination and marginalization for women.

CONTENTS

INTRODUCTION

On Halloween of 2016, I started a project that I named Feminist Mantra Monday. The idea was to create a weekly mantra series that would help people of all genders embrace feminisms and themselves as feminists. So each Monday for a year (with a few exceptions, of course), I posted a mantra on my Instagram profile and a brief essay explaining its meaning and feminist potential on my blog.

In many ways, the project was a public journaling process. The mantras were fueled by my activities and reflections from the week prior, often in response to things happening in the world at large. In other ways, however, the project took its own shape and form as readers invested their lives and meanings in the mantras and shared comments and conversations on my posts.

The mantras were always a self-exploratory prompt, but a community also blossomed around them. They became a collective rallying cry against the election of a sexist, white supremacist president; a reminder of the importance of activism and self-care in these times; and a signpost of the necessity of developing our deeply personal but always political feminist practice.

The intention of this book is to make space for each of us to continue (or to begin) a weekly feminist mantra practice in our lives. I encourage you to set aside a time each week to read and meditate on one of the mantras. They are arranged in the book by season, but feel free to skip weeks that don't resonate with you and come back when they do. There are also blank pages after each mantra to provide a space for you to make notes about how you see its application in your life and the lives of others.

It was an honor to share a year of feminist mantras and the dialogues that followed from them with such a rich and diverse community of followers. I am no longer posting mantras each week on Instagram, but this book is meant to continue and expand that community for the future.

If you make posts about the mantras or the book on your social profiles, feel free to tag them with **#50feministmantras**, and please never hesitate to be in touch to talk about your journey in feminist self-exploration and community-creation. It brings me true joy to take a part in it.

Always,
Amelia
@ladyameliaa

A NOTE ABOUT MANTRAS

Some of you may not be entirely familiar with the idea of mantras and their purpose. Most generally, mantras are words or phrases meant to be repeated to help you focus and concentrate. They are similar to intentions or guiding principles or very short prayers.

Each of the mantras in this book is just one or a few words long, and all of them start with verbs. The idea is that meditating on them will help them sink into your mind and heart, and then they will help guide your actions throughout the week. I find that in moments of stress or confusion, my weekly mantra can help me feel grounded in navigating our busy, complex world and making decisions that are true to myself.

There are many ways to develop a mantra practice. Some people like to meditate on their mantra each morning before they get out of bed. Others put a post-it note on their mirror or make it their phone background so that they see it many times a day. Some prefer to light a candle and journal about it once at the beginning of the week and then let it linger in their subconscious until the next week's mantra meditation.

I encourage you to craft a mantra practice that suits you and allows the mantras to best serve you. You may follow the writing prompts I give or make up your own as you go. There is no wrong way to use a mantra, and a mantra should always feel nourishing and supporting.

WINTER

i. BEGIN

A new year is always such an exciting thing. 365 days ahead of us to fill with adventures, desires, and dreams.

How do you feel today? Are you excited about what's to come? Still mourning something from the past? I find I'm always a bit of both minds as the new year begins. It may be a fresh start, but we never really get a clean break from everything that's come before.

If you're sitting down with this book, then you've decided that something about this year will be intentional. You will carve out space for yourself. You will seek and shape your identity. You will recognize that all of that happens amidst the challenging structures and systemic issues we face in the world.

The start of a new year is always an opportunity to begin. And a beginning, in some sense, is always a birth. It takes us back to the moments of our lives before we remember ourselves. It connects us to our mothers and the terrifying-glorifying moments of leaving a womb for the world. It represents a radical opening to possibility.

What possibilities do you seek this year? Make a list of what you desire for yourself, then another list of what you need from the world.

Are they different? The same? What begins today? What's one thing you can do today to seek something on your lists?

Try that thing. Tomorrow try another. Just begin.

ii. NURTURE YOUR HEART

How often do you stop and ask yourself what your heart needs?

Not what your body needs, or what you mind tells you, but what your heart needs, what the deep red organ of your emotions desires.

This week's mantra is about embracing the side of yourself that feels profoundly and working to articulate those feelings as desires that you respect and heed.

When do you feel most alive? When does your spirit overflow your body? When can you sense that surge of joy in your chest?

That's your heart speaking.

Write about the last moment you remember feeling that way.

What brought it on? How long has it been?

Nurturing your heart is about getting in touch with your deepest desires and manifesting them in the world.

It's a commitment to loving and respecting your erotic and emotional identities.

This week try to feel your heart in your chest. How does it beat? What does it tell you?

iii. BUILD STRENGTH

We build strength in physical, emotional, spiritual, or intellectual areas of our lives.

Building strength can mean lifting a heavier weight than you ever have or walking away from a relationship that you know in your gut needs to end. It can mean crafting a new meditation practice or learning a skill that has always intimidated you.

The most important thing to remember about building strength is that it doesn't happen all at once.

It happens bit by bit over time until suddenly you've become strong, perhaps without noticing.

Most often, women (and most marginalized people) are not encouraged to be strong in any of these ways.

But we are strong in all of them. And we can build even more strength in the upcoming months and years.

What's one area of your life where you feel particularly strong? What about another where you'd like to improve your strength? Is there a woman you'd like to emulate? Can her strength inspire yours?

Today, try to write down one area of your life where you'd like to find some strength.

Tomorrow brainstorm one thing you can do to feel stronger.

The next day, try to do it.

iv. DWELL

One of the beautiful things about
winter is that it is a time of
hibernation and rest in preparation
for bloom and blossom.

This mantra suggests that we accept
and embrace winter as a waiting
period.

First, we have to remember that
waiting isn't static or stagnant.

Rather, waiting provides a space for
stretching and reflecting. And
accepting waiting is about
embracing the present moment and
yourself in this moment.

Waiting also has an intimate
relationship with dwelling.

We dwell in our homes and our lives.
We take our time in each moment
and room.

In dwelling, we embrace a waiting that deepens.

Take extra time this week.

Try to pause throughout your routines and linger in those everyday movements and spaces.

Envision those routines now.

What's one moment you want to hold on to?

How can you resist the pressures of our capitalist society to always be working on something or towards the next thing?

How can you dwell in that moment you want to hold?

v. FEEL IN THE DARK

Our feelings are our most
genuine paths to knowledge.
— Audre Lorde

Most often, it seems like we spend
our time either too deep in our
feelings to make sense of them or
too far removed from them to think
anything but sensibly.

This feeling that we can only
succumb to or ignore our feelings is
a symptom of patriarchy and
patriarchy's emphasis on reason. We
aren't taught how to sense, process,
and value our emotions, so we are
either overwhelmed by them or out
of touch with them.

The scary thing about feelings is that
they seem to come from some dark
place inside of us that we can't make
sense of.

But what Audre Lorde reminds us is that those feelings may come from a dark place, but that place is generative, productive, and creative. That dark place gives birth to the things we know to be most true of ourselves.

How are you feeling today?

Write your answer in one or two sentences.

Close your eyes and ask again.

Write two or three sentences more.

Feel your way through that dark place.

Sense yourself there.

vi. TRUST THE PROCESS

Contemporary society encourages
us to be impatient. In our cultural
narratives of progress and efficiency,
we're always supposed to doing
more and doing it faster.

Often, however, life just doesn't
work this way.

So many things have to develop
slowly. So much has to take its time.

Rather than worrying about what
you're working toward this week, try
to consider how you're getting there.

What are the steps you're taking
and the stages you're moving
through?

How can you make each moment a
bit smoother, softer, more fulfilling?

How can you dwell in your process?

How can you trust where it takes you?

Trusting the process is also especially important for women, whose natural cycles and processes have been ignored or repressed for so long.

Don't let society make you believe that linear (phallic) processes of progress and endless growth are the only way.

Your process may be soft and circular and intuitive.

Seek out your cycle. Lean into it.

vii. EXPAND

Your playing small does not
serve the world. There is nothing
enlightened about shrinking so
that other people won't feel
insecure around you.
— Marianne Williamson

Somewhere in history, society
became obsessed with the idea of
women being small.

And that idea grew from an
obsession to a demand and from a
demand to a rule.

Now we're at the point where it
seems like women must be small;
they shouldn't take up space.

Not all women experience this in the
same way or even experience it at
all.

But it is a societal reality that all women have to confront and that all men need to refuse to comply with.

This week's mantra is a reminder of how positive it is to expand, to fill yourself out and grow bigger, larger, downright huge if you like, not necessarily in your body, but in your heart, mind and spirit.

Women are taught to take up less space, but what if women demanded more?

Take up all the space you can find today.

Make yourself an ocean.

See where your current takes you.

viii. COMFORT YOURSELF

Part of feminist consciousness is cultivating communities of women, listening to and embracing them.

Another, equally important, part of feminist consciousness is cultivating the ability to stand on your own and feel comfortable and confident in your skin and life.

This week focus on holding on to self-care routines and rituals that heal your spirit.

Building an intimate self-love practice is vital for survival, and it will make you better prepared to love others when they need to be comforted in turn.

A few self-comfort tools to start:
- Loose-leaf tea brewed slowly
- Mary Oliver poems
- Bouquets of eucalyptus & lavender
- New nail polish or lipstick
- Long walks that linger
- Your favorite dessert

And a few particularly feminist forms of self-comfort:
- Copying Audre Lorde essays into your journal
- Listening to Patti Smith albums
- Taking self-portraits
- Having a long conversation with a woman you admire

How can you comfort yourself this week?

Make a list of five different ways.

Accomplish that to-do list.

ix. GENERATE GOODWILL

> Goodwill is something you put away like preserves, for a rainy day, for winter, for lean times, and it was moving to find that I had more than I had ever imagined.
> — Rebecca Solnit

Winter often feels like a season of lean times.

But as much as we may miss the warmth of sunny days, this season is often also full of moments of gathering and community, of friends and family offering encouragement and support.

In winter, we have time and energy to spend time and energy cultivating and caring for our relationships. And when we need to call on them, those people and efforts will come back to us tenfold.

Like Rebecca Solnit said, there will be more goodwill than we can ever imagine.

To generate goodwill is to sow seeds of kindness, respect, and empathy with no expectation.

It is a refusal of the capitalist value structure that demands equal exchange, and the embrace of this fruitless labor that is so often labeled as feminine and ignored.

Most importantly, it is being proud of this work, valuing it and yourself, and knowing and trusting all the ways the goodwill you generate will return to you.

What can you do to generate goodwill this week?

What seeds will you sow?

x. STRETCH

Do you ever feel like everyone around you is pushing their boundaries and stepping outside their comfort zones? That you're watching the people you love stretch and grow?

Maybe some of them have taken it on voluntarily, and maybe others have been forced to try new things or new ways of doing things.

But regardless of the motive, that energy can make everything feel fresh and new.

This is one of the best things about an imminent change in seasons.

As it finally starts to feel like spring, we all start moving our bodies and stretching out again.

We make ourselves a bit uncomfortable, and we grow infinitely as a result.

This week, try to stretch.

Aim for something out of your reach, and see if you can grasp it.

It may be a raise, a new apartment, a challenging recipe, or, hell, even your toes.

Stretch and see where that new space takes you.

xi. STAY SEASONAL

In winter we tend to hibernate. We crave the warmth and comfort of blankets and hot beverages and one too many night-caps.

When the weather warms and days lighten, we crave greener foods and more outdoor activities. We fill spring full of salads and bike rides and long nights outside.

This is because Spring-You has different needs and desires than Winter-You. This is important to note and to remember that "bad" or "better" decisions are only bad or better in the context of the season you're making them in and whether or not they suit what your body and spirit need at the time.

The productive, abstract, rational world we live in tries to demand that our lives function without care for or appeal to the seasons, e.g. your boss expects you to be at work at 8am regardless of whether the sun rose at 5am or 7am.

This is largely the result of a patriarchal and capitalist value-system that demands we remain productive at the same rates year-round for maximum profit.

But in reality, our bodies and minds are in tune with our environments. Their needs and desires ebb and flow.

Stay seasonal is a reminder to listen to your body and give it what it needs with the understanding that these needs will fluctuate with the season. It's a call to tap into your feminine connection to Mother Earth.

How does the world feel to you lately?

What do you hope this season brings?

xii. WEIGH YOUR WEALTH

Your cup runneth over.
— Oprah

This week take stock of the
people/places/things in your life right
now. How much good can you find?

Has any negative thinking been
getting in the way of your
appreciating those good things
lately?

Focusing on the negative is a way of
focusing on everyone but yourself
and giving your attention to people
and things that don't deserve it.

Women are often told that the only
way to be strong is to be selfless
and give themselves to others. The
problem is that giving it all away is a
surefire way to have nothing left to
give.

Women can and should be strong, but in order to build strength, we don't need to be selfless but to be self-full.

Being self-full is giving ourselves to people/places/things that enrich and fulfill our lives.

So this week, try to refocus.

Meditate on all of the good things that have happened this week, this month, or this year.

How full is your cup? How can you stay full of this goodness?

This week weigh your wealth, and embrace this mantra as an exclamation of how much good is in your life and a reminder to keep that good energy in your life by not giving it to people and things that don't return it back to you.

SPRING

i. BREAK ROUTINE

A new season is a reminder to let go of the reins every so often to step outside of your day-to-day life.

Taking that brief moment away allows you to recalibrate your mind and your heart and return to your work with more intention and new clarity.

Breaking routine can be big or small.

It can mean leaving town and going on a national or international adventure.

Or it can be as simple as waking up early one morning rather than sleeping through the alarm, making coffee at home when you normally grab it on the run, or planning a special lunch date with a friend on a day you normally eat at your desk.

This week try to do one thing that is outside your norm.

Push yourself to give up a moment of work for a moment of reflection.

Hit refresh and reset your spirit.

What is that thing?

How can you do it?

ii. GROW SOFT

Normally we think of power as an outward show of strength, as an accumulation of money and knowledge, as a force to be reckoned with.

This is generally a phallic power that emphasizes traditionally masculine traits. This power's slogan might be go hard.

But soft power is power that is cultivated and grows on the inside. It's the strength you shore up in your spirit that shines through your smile as self-assurance.

It's a female or feminine or feminist power that attempts to redefine the traits we value in society. This power doesn't tell you to go hard, it tells you to grow soft.

This week's mantra is an exploration of the power that comes through self-knowledge and vulnerability.

It's about attending to each crack in our seams as a potential opening to the world rather than a dangerous flaw.

This will help us break down the walls that keep us from others rather than reinforcing them and building new ones.

What does grow soft mean to you all this week?

How can you grow softer?

iii. OPEN DOORS

What would happen if you opened every door in your life?

All of them.

Every single one you come across.

Like a kid when they go to a friend's house and immediately run around the whole place barging into every room.

This week try signing up for every class that sounds cool, showing up for every event your friends throw, and following up with every neat acquaintance you meet (maybe even some of the ones you met a while ago and never followed up with).

Put all your feelers out there and coffee-date your heart out.

We can't do everything all the time.

But for a week, we can remember to try new things and follow our gut down those long hallways of life.

The real living comes through the doors we throw open on a whim.

Later this spring, we'll get back to the reminders that there are also doors in your life that it's *really important* to shut.

But for now, trying opening a few.

Where could they take you?

iv. ENACT YOUR EMOTIONS

One of the most important lessons we can learn from feminist activists and theorists is that feelings matter and that often our most challenging feelings are our most important ones.

Historically, emotions are dismissed in favor of reason (aka "crazy" women written off in favor of "rational" men).

But life is often so much more affective than it is logical.

It's the feelings we're having that are going to create the change we wish to see in the world (hi, Gandhi, what's up) just as much as it is the ideas we have about how to change it.

The important thing is to enact your emotions.

And sometimes our emotions enact us straight to the bathtub with a bottle of wine.

But there's more than that.

There are **protests** and **letter-writing campaigns** and **conflict resolution training**.

Our emotions need to take us to those places as often as they do to the bathtub.

This week express your emotions with purpose.

Channel your feelings into something larger than yourself.

v. AMPLIFY

An important aspect of feminist consciousness is learning to listen, empathize and be an ally.

What does it mean to be an ally exactly?

It means listening and empathizing.

It means seeking out opportunities to hear marginalized voices and paying close attention to what they say.

It means recognizing and accounting for your privilege and understanding the structural and systemic entities that may oppress others.

Once you do that, it means amplifying those voices and making sure they're heard.

In many cases, those voices may be your own.

You may be the one who needs to be heard.

Being an ally is understanding whose voice must be amplified when and taking the time to figure that out.

Do that work, then the premise is simple: show up and shout.

vi. FIND YOUR LIGHT

Light is the left hand of darkness
and darkness the right hand of
light.
Two are one, life and death,
lying
together like lovers in kemmer,
like hands joined together,
like the end and the way.
— Ursula Le Guin

How does the world feel lately?
Light or dark? Full of possibility or
challenge?

Because of the way that night and
day seem to alternate, we tend to
think of light and dark as mutually
exclusive, as either one or the other.

In certain sense, however, this is a
fallacy.

It's not that day is light and night is dark, but that each rotation of the earth is the slipping within and between the two, that light and dark mingle in every hour, hand in hand.

This is a hard lesson to hold, but one that can bring a lot of peace when embraced.

The task of this week is to learn to dwell in the darkness.

The darkness of not knowing what will come next. The darkness of not knowing how to proceed. The darkness of not being sure who is close to us and how to reach them, let alone how to help those who feel and are so far away.

Spend a few days in the dark.

What clarity do you find? What light starts to shine?

Find it.

vii. CRAFT COMMUNITY

Our patriarchal capitalist society tells us that we should have a do-it-yourself mentality.

We have to be individuals and accomplish everything on our own. When we succeed we get all the glory. And when we fail, it's all on us.

But a feminist perspective emphasizes community and the role that others play in all of our decisions and actions.

Our successes and failures belong to the people that love, support, and praise us as much as they belong to any one of us individually.

No single person can do everything.

It's never all on us.

That said, one person can craft a network that allows them to create meaningful change with widespread impact.

An individual can change the world.

But they're never doing it alone.

This week meditate on these questions:

  - Do you have real community in your life? What does real community mean to you?

  - Are there women you turn to for advice? For comfort? Who are they?

  - How do these women inspire and impress you? How do you inspire and impress them?

  - How can you cultivate these relationships? How can you craft a better community?

viii. PERSIST

> You are not obligated to
> complete the work, but neither
> are you free to abandon it.
> — Rabbi Tarfon

Giving up is tempting sometimes,
isn't it?

Some tasks present so many
obstacles that appear so large that
abandoning them all together seems
like the only option.

This week's mantra is a reminder
that some storms appear large but
pass quickly and others we have to
ride out for the long haul.

Either way, we'll never know what
type of storm we're in unless we
persist through it. And we can't see
the rainbow until we're on the
other side.

Persistence teaches us about our strengths.

We learn our true potential when we push past the moments where we want to give up.

What is something you've been struggling with or frustrated about lately?

Are you feeling stuck in any area of your life?

Make a list of what comes to mind.

What things on the list seem worth sitting in the rain?

How can you persist a little longer?

What strength will you find on the other side of that moment?

ix. SHARE LOVE

One of the best ways we can resist our white-supremacist, capitalist, patriarchal society is to care for, about, and with each other.

Our most powerful tool of resistance is cultivating love among ourselves.

In our culture, we often think of love as a romantic grand gesture, but more often it is embedded in small moments of care that we offer to people we do or don't know in our everyday lives.

Make a list of people you love.

In a second column, write down one way you've cared for each of those people recently.

How have you shown them love and shared love with them?

Now make a list of people you
encounter in your daily life.

Think particularly about those you'd
considered strangers.
Are there ways you can care for
them as well?

How can you share love with those
people?

Make a list of acts of kindness and
gratitude that you can offer the
people around you.

Carry the list with you throughout
the week.

Check things off as you go.

x. RETURN HOME

How long has it been since you went home?

Is home a place for you? Or maybe a person?

Home most often seems to be a feeling.

Where do you find it?

This week find a way to return to that feeling.

Maybe you reach out to a person who knew you when you were younger or when you felt most like yourself.

Maybe you visit a part of town you spent a lot of time in when you first lived there.

Maybe you make a meal your mother made you growing up.

Home likely means different things to each of us, but it is also a powerful, grounding force.

We all share the Earth as our home.

We all tend and care for it and ourselves as inhabitants of it.

If nothing comes to mind as home this week, find a way to return to the earth.

Walk barefoot in soil or sand.

Remember where you've come from.

Return there.

xi. DEFINE DESIRE

> Oh heart, now that I know your
> nature,
> who can I tell?
> — Margaret Atwood

As humans, we are full of desires.
Sunshine. Sex. Pizza. We want so
many things.

We often think of the opposite of
desire as discipline. We believe we
can control our desires if we are
disciplined enough.

We're even taught to do so and
encouraged to be ascetic, abstaining
from bodily pleasure and embracing
the life of the mind.

We work to take hold of and limit
our desires, making sure our rational
needs take precedent over our
emotional/embodied wants.

But desire is a deeply erotic and feminine power.

In developing a feminist consciousness, the goal is not to discipline desire, but to learn to define what and how we desire.

We shouldn't take control of our desires by limiting them.

We should embrace them by learning to articulate them.

This week make a list of things you want.

What do you desire?

How specific can you be?

How can these desires play a larger role in your daily life?

xii. WRITE YOUR SELF

And why don't you write? Write!
Writing is for you, you are for
you; your body is yours, take it.
— Hélène Cixous

Throughout history, women have
used words to share their
experiences and selves.

From Sojourner Truth to Virginia
Woolf and Sylvia Plath to bell hooks,
women have turned to language to
make sense of their lives and to
claim space in the world.

They've used words to speak their
bodies and truths aloud.

Have you ever written your story?

Have you shared a scene or told it
from start to finish?

This week take a moment to start that process.

Write a single scene or many scenes.

Start at the beginning or in the middle.

Maybe you do this alone at home with pen and paper, or in crowded coffee shop on your laptop.

Maybe you start telling the story in conversation with someone you care about or in speech to a room full of people.

No matter how you do it, begin writing yourself.

Find the words.

Your story is yours, take it.

xii. CARRY A TALISMAN

As spring slips into summer,
consider crafting a ritual to associate
with the change of season.

What is one thing you hope to
manifest this summer?

What do you hope to accomplish?

What do you hope the universe will
provide for you?

Write down a few thoughts in
response to each of these questions.

Meditate on your answers.

Does any particular image come to
mind?

Find a small talisman to represent this image and the things you hope to manifest in the upcoming season.

Maybe it's a stone or a crystal, a photo or a keychain.

Try to choose something small that you can carry with you throughout the summer.

Draw a picture of it here.

Let it hold your dreams.

Hold it tight.

SUMMER

i. REFRESH

The start of summer always marks the halfway point of the year.

You've survived, maybe even thrived, and there's still half a year ahead!

Take a few moments this week to check in with yourself and what you need from the rest of the year.

If you're working through this mantra practice chronologically, turn back to your notes from early in the year and see what has shifted.

Have you accomplished things you meant to?

Have you let go of or embraced certain feelings?

What feels old and what feels new?

How can you reevaluate and recommit to your goals?

Write answers to each of these questions, then ask yourself:

What would it mean to hit refresh on your life right now?

Can you identify one area of your life that needs a refresh the most?

Set a concrete refresh goal and three steps for enacting it.

ii. DEMAND FREEDOM

> Freedom is never voluntarily
> given by the oppressor; it must
> be demanded by the oppressed.
> — Martin Luther King, Jr.

What does it mean to you to be free?

Is freedom a political right? A social cause? A personal endeavor?

Freedom certainly is an important political right to claim and reality to fight for.

It's also an affective dimension of our lives. Freedom is something we must have and feel.

This week meditate on what it means to you to *feel* free in your daily life and your relationships.

What does freedom feel like in your gut? Your heart?

What conditions have to be true for you to feel free?

Be gentle yet firm with yourself in this exploration.

What stands out as flexible and what is non-negotiable?

Once you have a sense of how you feel free, spend some time with Martin Luther King, Jr.'s words.

What would it mean for you to demand this feeling?

How can you seek and cultivate freedom in your life? And assist others in their search?

iii. BLOW IT UP

I hope as I get older and scared-
er that I don't forget how to
blow up my life and start over
and over again.
— Mitski

When was the last time you made a
radical change in your life?

How often do you blow something
up and start over?

This week imagine what it would be
like to take a sharp left in your life.

Is there a dream you've never
followed? A person you've never
reached out to? A path left
untraveled?

What would happen if you turned
toward that dream/person/path?

Consider taking that leap.

How would taking that leap feel?

Scary, to be sure.

But also invigorating, enlivening,
maybe even freeing.

Make a list of everything in your life
you could or might want to blow up.

Make a list of how you'd feel if
you did.

Is joy anywhere on that list?

Chase it.

iv. FORGIVE

Forgiveness is a fickle endeavor.

It's something we often seek to have
or to give, but it seems tenuous and
unclear.

How can we forgive? What does
that mean?

Part of the challenge of forgiveness
is that forgiveness presupposes that
something 'wrong' has been done
and the nature of that wrong-doing
presupposes that something else
'should' have been done.

How do we know what we should
do in our own lives or for others?

We often rely on rules and laws to
determine these 'shoulds'.

But how often do we feel like
someone has done something

wrong without being able to point to the exact rule that's been broken?

This week's mantra is about meditating on the things you believe you should be doing in your life and what you think others around you should be doing.

How can you define those 'shoulds' more clearly?

Which ones do you need to let go?

Focus on forgiving yourself for a slip-up or all-out abandonment of those things you think you 'should' be doing.

Try to forgive someone else for the same. Invent new boundaries and agreements that you craft intentionally.

v. RUN WILD

Women have been associated with
the wild for most of human history.

What it means to be female or
feminine is attached to a deeply
human sense of embodiment and
desire.

To the birth of all life.

To the womb that is the deep, dark
space we emerge from but never
quite remember.

That's what the wild is after all.

A purely generative darkness.

A space our minds can't quite make
sense of where our bodies take
charge.

What images are conjured up when you meditate on the words 'run wild'?

How do they shift when you image yourself running wild?

This week infuse your life with more wildness.

How can you return to that deep, dark space of yourself?

How can you carry that space into the light of the world?

vi. SIT IN THE MESS

Our society places a high value on progress. Everything and everyone should always be moving forward and getting better.

This is a fairly phallic, masculine premise. That everything must be up and pointed ahead all the time.

Life doesn't necessarily work that way.

Nature moves cyclically, circling back around to and through the same four seasons and many moon cycles as time passes.

Because of this societal valuing of the progressive over the cyclical, when something goes awry in life, we tend to work hard to push past it. We want to move forward and move on as quickly as possible.

Sometimes, however, we need to stay in those moments of discomfort.

We need to linger in that shitty space and see how it takes shape. We need to sit in the mess.

What's one area of your life or the life of someone close to you that may not be going as planned right now?

How can you sit in the mess with yourself or with them?

We can you learn from making space there?

vii. DEVOTE YOURSELF

Why do you write? A chorus
erupts.
Because we cannot simply live.
— Patti Smith

Patti Smith titled her book on writing
Devotion.

Throughout the book, an important
theme is the way that writing
becomes an all-encompassing task.
That it's something we're taken in by
and must give ourselves to.

When was the last time you got
caught up in a project or endeavor
with such a fervent pleasure that
you forgot about everything else?

When was the last time you devoted
yourself to something so fully that
the world beyond it just fell away?

This week meditate on an idea or dream that you could imagine devoting yourself to.

Maybe it's a book, a business, or a band.

Make notes and sketches.

Outline steps and processes.

How does it feel to get swept up in those plans?

Could you make them a reality?

viii. MOVE YOUR GIFT

What does it mean to live in a
capitalist economy?

It means living in a world where our
lives are valued by our productive—
or for women, reproductive—
abilities. It means judging ourselves
and others by how much material
wealth we accumulate.

In a capitalist world, there is never
enough, and we can never have
enough. Everything must be ours.

How can we have enough without
holding on to too much? How can
we do good work, feel good about
our work, and "make a living" as we
call it?

In the face of these questions, we
may find ourselves holding too
tightly to the things we have, feeling
like there's too little and wondering

how to get more. This is called a scarcity mindset.

In the midst of tightening our grip, however, we need to reflect on how frequently people are willing to give and how abundantly they share.

Living in society of scarcity makes it even more important to look around and realize how often there is plenty. And then we have to share. And we have to share a little more than we think we can. And trust that it will come back to us in turn.

This is what it means to move your gift. To share what you can and a little more. To trust that it will return to you.

Where can you find abundance in your life this week?

How can you share it?

ix. REST TOGETHER

Normally we think of resting as something that happens in solitude.

Rest is sleeping in on a Sunday morning. It's painting your nails or taking a bath.

But sometimes during those times our minds wander back to whatever has been bothering us. Perhaps we mull over negative thoughts or return to painful memories.

So even though we may not be doing anything, we don't actually rest.

Even though we think of rest as a solitary endeavor, it can also be a deeply communal activity.

We can rest together at a yoga class or in a movie theater. We can take long walks with friends or linger on the phone for hours.

Sometimes resting with others allows us to get out of our heads enough for the cobwebs to clear and clarity to take their place.

This week find your people and spend time just spending time with them.

Allow that rest to motivate you to work harder and better toward your goals.

x. SET BOUNDARIES

Our society tends to always be asking us for more. Especially those of us that are women.

We're expected to give our time, our energy, our care, and our attention to everyone all the time. And we're rarely applauded for offering any of those things to ourselves.

In order to resist this, we have to set boundaries, and one helpful way to set boundaries is to develop personal policies.

How do you make personal policies? It's fairly straightforward:

> Come up with a list of things you immediately wish you had said no to every single time you say yes to them.

Rewrite that list, starting each item with "I have a personal policy against _____."

The exact personal policy you develop is flexible, what's important is that you use personal policies to set boundaries that (a) eliminate anxiety and (b) help you move toward your goals and happiness in life.

The trick for using personal policies is to develop them in advance and to always say that they're *personal policies* when you use them; for example "No, thank you. I have a personal policy against _____."

It can be hard to say at first, but personal policies incite respect for boundary-setting and strength. People will be impressed.

This week brainstorm a list of new personal policies. Put one or two into action. You won't regret it.

xi. LABOR LESS

The start of September celebrates
the birth of the US labor movement
which worked to do things like
create an 8-hour work day and
protect workers' rights to
compensation and safe working
conditions.

This week check in with the type,
intensity, and amount of labor you're
doing lately.

Are you working too much? Too
little?

Remember that labor isn't just your
"job."

Are you laboring for wealth? health?
friends? family?

What aspects of your life don't feel
like work?

How can you lean into those places and spaces that don't feel like work?

If at any point in your reflection something feels "too much," meditate on how you can labor less in that area.

How can you transform the work so it does feel like work or invest your energy elsewhere in your life?

How can you labor less?

xii. SEEK CRITIQUE

An important part of feminist consciousness is the development of our female and feminine selves, the embracing of aspects of our lives and humanity that are crushed by a patriarchal society.

An equally important part of feminist consciousness, though, is also being open to feedback on how we can do better, particularly how we can be better community members and allies.

This week find small ways to seek feedback on your ideas and actions.

Approach these conversations from a vulnerable place and be open to what you hear.

When you do so, be sure to identify people who will offer critique from a place of care rather than malice.

Make a list of these caring people now.

Take notes during or after you speak to them.

Take their words to heart.

xiii. SET NEW PATTERNS

As humans, we seem to develop habits and routines.

We go through our day to day lives speaking to the same people, driving the same routes, and visiting the same places.

There's a lot of comfort in these habits and routines.

They help us cope with the scary invariability of the world we live in which often seems chaotic and overwhelming.

But our habits and routines can also be enticing forms of comfort that keep us from growing and fulfilling our potentials.

They can keep us stuck in states we may not intentionally be entering.

This week meditate on what habits and routines you hold fast to in your life.

Do you have coffee every morning? Do you park in the same place each day at work?

Become aware of your habits. Make mental and physical notes of them.

When you're more conscious of the habits you have, consider which ones you might change.

Could you become a tea drinker two days a week? Might you walk to work or park your car elsewhere?

Where can you invite new patterns into your life?

Choose at least one routine to experiment with this week. Try something new.

FALL

i. ASK

Are you the kind of person that asks for help?

Are you comfortable reaching out to friends or strangers when you need assistance? When was the last time you did so?

Our culture places a high value on self-sufficiency. We're supposed to do everything ourselves.

Community, according to our society, is just a plus, something we find if we're lucky.

It may be counterintuitive, then, that one of the best ways to build community is to ask people to help.

When asking for help, you have to come from a place of vulnerability and care, a place of trust in yourself and the other person or people.

Within each ask there should be an offer embedded. The offer of care and gratitude, of joining a community larger than oneself in which both the one who asks and the one who helps find fulfillment.

If you ask in this way, people want to help and offer support. They want to come together to assist you.

This week think about something you could use help with.

Who can you ask for help? How can you ask them?

Carry a spirit of asking for help with you throughout the week.

What do you end up asking?

Who do you end up assisting?

ii. EVOLVE

Following your heart also means
eliminating the things that no
longer evolve you.
— Erykah Badu

How have you grown this year?
What feels new and different?

As fall takes hold of the world,
reflect on what aspects of your own
life still feel fresh and green and
which are feeling wilted.

Does anything feel rather stale? Are
there people, places, or things you've
outgrown?

Sometimes evolving is graceful and
the things we've outgrown fade and
fall like leaves from trees.

But other times, the process of evolving can be painful, like repotting a plant that loves its container.

What's important to remember is that true flourishing is on the other side.

Take some time this week to meditate on what pillars in your life may be holding you in place more than propelling you forward.

Can you afford to let them go?

Don't be afraid to evolve.

iii. STAY IN TOUCH

This week's mantra is a reminder to reach out to someone you've known for a long time, even if it's been ages.

Give them a call. Write them an email. Send a small gift.

People from our past help us see the clearest images of ourselves.

As we speak with them, they reflect our shine (and our tarnish) back to us.

They show us ourselves as we are, because we can't see our growth on our own. It takes an outside perspective to remind us how much has really changed.

So this week, try to rekindle a relationship.

Tell a person from your past what they once meant to you. Tell them what they mean now. Make a plan for keeping in touch in the future.

As you get (and stay) in touch, remember that the bonds we maintain are our strongest resistance to the neoliberal, capitalist world that isolates us and pits us (especially women) against each other.

These relationships are important. Personally and politically.

Who have you lost touch with?

How can you become close again?

iv. KNOW YOUR POWER

Have you embraced the power pose?

Hands on hips. Feet slightly wider than hip-width apart. Chest out. Head tilted to the sky.

Try it now. Stand up and power pose.

Hold the position for 30 seconds at least. How does it feel?

This week's task is to reflect on how powerful you are. Consider these questions:

- Do you think of yourself as powerful?
- What makes you feel powerful?
- When do you feel powerful?
- How can you feel more powerful?
- What makes your power uniquely your own?

Carry this final question with you throughout the week.

Take note of the moments you feel powerful.

How you can cultivate more of those moments in your life?

v. NEST

Associating femininity with domesticity has been one of the most powerfully oppressive tools of our patriarchal society.

We're told that women are supposed to be quiet, toe the line, and *stay home*; that's their place.

In an effort to rebuke this nonsensical argument, feminists have fought hard for women's rights to leave home and seek success in the world.

Over the past two centuries, women have (somewhat) liberated themselves from the cult of domesticity, and feminists are still doing important work to maintain and extend women's newfound and hard-earned rights.

Somehow in this fight, however, domesticity became maligned, and the home became a contested space.

In leaving their homes, women also often lost their homes. Space became strange.

This week's mantra invites you to come full circle by simultaneously embracing being liberated from domesticity *and* cultivating a private space.

Find a place for yourself this week and make it your own. Maybe you rearrange your bookshelf. Maybe you light a new candle. Maybe you clean off your desktop.

Put a personal touch on a place you often find yourself.

Nest a bit there. Find comfort in it.

vi. GET A LITTLE WITCHY

There is a long history of femininity
being associated with magic.

In some eras, this gives women
great political power, in others, it
leads to their violent deaths.

No matter the political or historical
differences, women's association
with magic reflects a general cultural
consciousness of a deeply
mysterious and deeply feminine
power in the world that emanates
from Mother Earth and takes root in
every human.

Getting witchy means embracing the
unknown in life, stepping into the
darkness with courage, and trusting
that the world will send you what
you need.

It's also a call toward the mystical
and magical.

Check in with your horoscope this week. Pop down to Chinatown and have your aura read. Ask a friend to do a tarot reading.

Seek knowledge that comes from a mystical place.

Don't let the bright light of modern science make you turn away from the darkness.

Instead embrace its power and tap into the strength of our female ancestors.

Channel their voices into your own and take time this week to claim the healing you deserve.

vii. EMBRACE VULNERABILITY

Have you ever looked up synonyms for vulnerability?

The dictionary lists the following: defenseless, exposed, liable, unsafe, weak, naked, unguarded, sucker.

Vulnerability is a quality often associated with femininity.

Society tells us that women are more vulnerable than men and that they must act accordingly.

And while it is important to note the real dangers that women face in a society that sees their bodies as assailable, sexualized objects, it is also important to refuse the negative connotations that then get assigned to words like 'vulnerability.'

We have to rewrite the dictionaries that tell us that feminine qualities are weak and make us defenseless.

We have to make the world see that those qualities are our greatest strengths. And doing that starts with experiencing them as strengths ourselves.

So this week, challenge yourself to say something, share something, or do something that makes you feel vulnerable.

Take a risk with a community you trust and see where it leads you.

viii. RECOGNIZE EMOTIONAL LABOR

One important feminist effort is to make visible the forms of invisible labor that women (and others) do in their personal and professional lives.

This labor is often called "emotional labor."

Examples of emotional labor include helping colleagues through relationship issues because they feel like they can talk to you, handling twice as many emails as a peer because people feel like you're more "approachable," or being expected to plan and pick up after a monthly work social because "women are good that those things."

This week try to keep track of your unnoticed emotional labor (or the labor of women around you).

Note the things you do that are crucial to keep so many things running but often get swept under the rug.

How can you make that labor more visible?

Do you have allies in your work and life that can help you recognize that labor publically?

ix. TAKE A DEEP BREATH

How often do you think about
breathing?

Take a deep breath right now.

Then another.

How does it feel?

What words do you have to describe
your breathing? Write them down.

Breathing is an incredibly crucial but
entirely mundane aspect of our lives.
As such, we often forget about it.

This week try to focus on your
breath.

Is it slower in the morning?

Does it get more shallow when you
drink three cups of coffee?

How does breathing feel when you exercise?

Try to pause a few times a day and take a deep breath.

What do you inhale in those moments?

What do you exhale?

x. GIVE THANKS

Take time this week to make a list of all the people in your life that you are thankful for.

Who are they?

How have they helped you?

How can you thank them?

After you make the list, choose a few names that stand out to you.

Sometime this week, go to a stationary store and buy nice cards and a pen.

Write thank you notes to the people you chose.

Tell them how much you appreciate them.

Share a memory of them that warms your heart.

Give thanks for them and give them your thanks.

xi. CULTIVATE STILLNESS

Do you often find your mind flitting
from place to place unable to focus?
Does it wander every time you have
a free moment?

What about your body? Do your legs
twitch as you sit at your desk or your
hands wander as you try to type?

Our culture tends to suggest that we
should always be on the move.

We value active minds and bodies in
motion. Stillness and slowness is
branded as dull and lazy.

But what if we refused those
associations?

We can challenge the cultural idea
that we must always be progressing
in favor of finding peace in staying in
place.

When was the last time you felt you were truly still?

Take a few moments this week to sit still.

Maybe you find a local yoga or meditation class.

Maybe you make time to sit in the dark each morning.

Find a stillness in your body that your mind can follow.

xii. CLOSE DOORS

As the year comes to a close, it's important to reflect on what else in your life may naturally be coming to an end.

What seems to be wrapping up?

Think about your work, your friendships, your personal projects.

What is finishing right now or what can you bring to a finish?

Take some time to write answers to these questions.

When the new year begins, it will be important to have enough space in your life for new ideas and possibilities.

The only way to make that space is to close a few doors now.

xiii. CREATE IN THE DARK

Creation is always in the dark because you can only do the work of making by not quite knowing what you're doing, by walking into darkness, not staying in the light. Ideas emerge from edges and shadows to arrive in the light, and though that's where they may be seen by others, that's not where they're born.
— Rebecca Solnit

As the days grow shorter, there's more darkness in the world.

Darkness seems terrifying and intimidating. But now you've spent a year learning of its deep, feminine power.

How can you walk into the darkness as the year ends?

What will you bring back to the light?

CLOSING

In preparing this book, I wrote a feminist mantra every Monday for over a year. When I sat down to compile and edit this volume, I was amazed at how quickly I was able to revise old mantras and write new ones. It felt like in my year of writing, I had built up my 'mantra muscle' and the meditations came faster and easier than they did in the beginning.

If you've worked through this book, then you've strengthened your mantra muscle as well. You've reflected on your feminine and feminist self and, hopefully, come to enlightening and empowering conclusions.

Read back through some of your notes from the earliest mantras, then some from the middle of the book, and a few from the end. What has changed? What have you learned?

Before you move into the new year, practice writing a few mantras for yourself here.

Maybe you write a mantra for the next week, month, and season. Maybe you write a mantra for winter, spring, summer, and fall. Maybe you allow your mind to wander and see what words come.

Try to find words that suit your intentions. Focus on verbs that can guide your actions.

Use the blank page after this to brainstorm new mantras. Choose one or a few to be the themes of the next year. Start chanting them daily.

Thank you for joining me on this journey in feminist community. It's a joy to guide and travel beside you.

Always,
Amelia

RESOURCES
(in no particular order)

Sister Outsider, Audre Lorde

Feminism is for Everybody, bell hooks

The Art of Asking, Amanda Palmer

A Field Guide to Getting Lost, Rebecca Solnit

The Faraway Nearby, Rebecca Solnit

Men Explain Things to Me, Rebecca Solnit

Tiny Beautiful Things, Cheryl Strayed

"The Gift Must Always Move," Lewis Hyde

Selected Poems II, Margaret Atwood

Many Moons workbooks

Just Kids, Patti Smith

Devotion, Patti Smith

Trying to Make the Personal Political: Feminism and Consciousness-Raising, Half Letter Press

"The Laugh of the Medusa," Helene Cixous

Goddesses in Everywoman: Powerful Archetypes in Women's Lives, Jean Shinoda Bolen

Women Who Run With the Wolves, Clarissa Pinkola Estés, Ph.D.

MANTRA INDEX

Winter

Start fresh
Nurture your heart
Build strength
Dwell
Feel in the dark
Trust the process
Expand
Comfort yourself
Generate goodwill
Stretch
Stay seasonal
Weigh your wealth

Spring

Break routine
Grow soft
Open doors
Enact your emotions
Amplify
Find your light
Craft community
Persist
Share love
Return home
Define desire
Write your self
Carry a talisman

Summer

Refresh
Demand freedom
Blow it up
Forgive
Run wild
Sit in the mess
Devote yourself
Move your gift
Rest together
Set boundaries
Labor less
Seek critique
Set new patterns

Fall

Ask
Evolve
Stay in touch
Know your power
Nest
Get a little witchy
Embrace vulnerability
Recognize emotional
 labor
Take a deep breath
Give thanks
Cultivate stillness
Close doors
Create in the dark

ACKNOWLEDGEMENTS

All my love to my friends, family, and followers who supported this project. Special thanks to Emily Jones for a million delicious meals and the brilliant cover design. Particular appreciation to Wilco, my cat companion.

ABOUT THE AUTHOR

Amelia Hruby writes, podcasts, and builds communities of powerful women in Chicago, IL. Find her on the internet at @ladyameliaa.

Made in the USA
Lexington, KY
08 January 2018